THE
EVERYTHING™
WEDDING
VOWS
BOOK

THE EVERYTHING™ WEDDING VOWS BOOK

*Janet Anastasio and
Michelle Bevilacqua
Illustrated by
Kimberly Young*

ADAMS MEDIA CORPORATION
Holbrook, Massachusetts

An Everything™ Series book.
The Everything™ Series is a trademark of
Adams Media Corporation.

Published by Adams Media Corporation
260 Center Street, Holbrook, MA 02343

ISBN: 1-55850-364-1

Printed in Canada.

J   I   H   G   F   E   D

Library of Congress Number: 94-231811

COVER DESIGN: Barry Littmann

*This book is available at quantity discounts for bulk purchases.
For information, call 1-800-872-5627
(in Massachusetts 617-767-8100).*

Visit our home page at http://www.adamsmedia.com

DEDICATION

To your life together as husband and wife.

CONTENTS

ACKNOWLEDGMENTS

The authors wish to express their grateful thanks to the staffs of the Holbrook Public Library of Holbrook, Massachusetts, and the Flint Public Library of Middleton, Massachusetts. Special thanks to Peter Gouck for his patience and cooperation through the design process of this book.

INTRODUCTION

So—you're looking for something different to say at the altar, an alternative to the traditional wedding vows. THE EVERYTHING WEDDING VOWS BOOK will point you toward the perfect vow for you and your fiancé. Whether you want to create a unique vow for the two of you, adopt a nontraditional vow that seems perfect for your situation, or incorporate a favorite poem or song into your exchange, you'll find plenty of inspiration in these pages.

If you decide to write your own vows, start by considering what is important to both of you. What things do you share and value as a couple? What goals in life do you share? You're in charge—so customize the proceedings to your own interests and dreams. Think of your wedding vows as a film: You and your partner are the writer, director and producer. Use the advice that follows as a blueprint, but let your imagination run wild!

In planning your ceremony, you may also want to include some supplementary readings, such as passages from the Bible, poems, or other readings from other sources on the subject of love and marriage. You'll find plenty of source material here.

— Janet Anastasio
Michelle Bevilacqua

CHAPTER 1:
A FEW WORDS ABOUT
CREATING YOUR OWN
WEDDING VOWS

Important note: before you get too far along in the process of creating a personalized vow—and before you get too attached to what you've created—check with your ceremony officiant for guidelines on how to proceed. Different traditions take different approaches on the question of what should or should not be said at the altar. Be sure to resolve all important issues along these lines early on in the process. You don't want to have to make changes at the last minute!

If you are considering developing your own wedding vow, it's probably because

you want to formalize your commitment with something unique, something that is specific to your relationship or situation. You want the words you say on the big day to mean something that is truly meaningful to both of you. This is not to say that the traditional vows aren't special or meaningful—but vows you create yourself will be more personalized.

You should feel free to incorporate the location of your wedding into your vows. For instance, if you and your fiancé are planning a ceremony on or near the water, perhaps on a sailboat or at a seaside resort, you might want to incorporate this in some way in your wedding vows. In Chapter Two, you will find several sets of verses that can be adapted to weddings on or near the water, as well as dozens of other verses that may be appropriate for your situation. You may decide the very best way to emphasize the importance of the location to you and your guests is for you and your partner to compose an original poem of your own.

Some Guidelines

When creating your own vows, start by writing down answers to the following questions. Doing so will provide you with valuable source material—and help you develop the vow you're looking for:

Answer together: How do you, as a couple, define the following terms?

Love: _____

_____

_____

_____

Trust: _____

_____

_____

_____

Marriage: _____

_____

_____

_____

_____

Family: _____

_____

_____

_____

_____

Commitment: _____

_____

_____

_____

_____

Togetherness: _____

_____

_____

_____

_____

_____

Answer together: How did the two of you first meet?

_____

_____

_____

_____

_____

Answer separately: What was the first thing you noticed about your partner?

Bride: _____

_____

_____

_____

_____

Groom: _____

_____

_____

_____

_____

Answer together: List here any shared hobbies or other mutual interests you have.

_____

_____

_____

_____

Answer together: What was the single most important event in your relationship? (Or, what was the event that you feel says the most about your development as a couple?)

_____

_____

_____

_____

Answer together: How similar (or different) were your respective childhoods? Take a moment and try to recount some of the important parallels or differences here.

_____

_____

_____

_____

_____

Answer together: Is there a song, poem, or book that is particularly meaningful in your relationship? If so, identify it here.

_____

_____

_____

Answer together: Do you and your partner share a common religious tradition? If so, identify it here.

_____

_____

_____

Answer together: If you share a common religious tradition, is there a particular scriptural passage that you as a couple find particularly meaningful? If so, identify it here.

_____

_____

_____

_____

Answer together: How do you and your partner look at personal growth and change? What aspects of your life together are likely to change over the coming years? How do you anticipate dealing with those changes? How important is mutual respect and tolerance in your relationship? When one of you feels that a particular need is being overlooked, what do you feel is the best way to address this problem with the other person?

_____

_____

_____

_____

Answer together: Do you and your partner have a common vision of what your life as older people will be like? Will it include children or grandchildren? Take this opportunity to put into words the vision you and your partner share of what it will be like to grow old together.

_____

_____

_____

_____

Using the material you have developed, set about the task of writing a first draft of your unique wedding vow.

Let yourself go—there is no right or wrong way to write your wedding vow. Give yourself permission to write anything and everything that seems right—you can always cut text back later on. Don't be surprised if it takes you a few drafts to develop a vow that is right for you.

You need not follow any particular form or pattern, but if you feel more comfortable doing so, you may want to consider working within one of the following outlines.

Outline One

GROOM:
(Initial statement relating to past.)

BRIDE:
(Initial statement relating to past.)

GROOM:
(Statement relating to partner.)

BRIDE:
(Statement
relating to
partner.)

GROOM:
(Promise or
commitment in
terms you feel
are appropriate
for your
relationship.)

BRIDE:
(Promise or commitment in terms you feel are
appropriate for your relationship.)

Example:

GROOM:
When I was a child, I thought nothing would
ever persuade me leave my home state of
Maine when it came time to make my way in
the world. But that was before I met you.

BRIDE:
As a young girl, I dreamed of a place
where I could grow with another, step by
step, side by side. I have found that place in
your heart.

GROOM:
Kathy, you have helped me to learn that love
is a direction, and not a destination.

BRIDE:
John, you have taught me that when someone is there, no matter what, trust and commitment come without effort, of their own accord.

GROOM:
J pledge to you my future. J will share all my tomorrows with you and no other.

BRIDE:
J pledge to you my future. J will share all my tomorrows with you and no other.

Outline Two

GROOM:
(Extended statement incorporating important materials developed in answering the questions _above_, and culminating in a statement of your commitment to one another.)

BRIDE:
(Extended statement incorporating important materials developed in answering the questions _above_, and culminating in a statement of your commitment to one another.)

Example:

GROOM:
The first thing J noticed about Kathy was her radiant smile. We were both auditioning for a show in college, and when J asked her what

type of piece she'd prepared, she said she planned to make it all up on the spot—and then she smiled at me. Kathy, your warmth and spontaneity have won my heart utterly. From this day forward, I will stand by your side. You are the one I will be true to always. Let us make our lives together.

BRIDE:

The first thing I noticed about John was his unceasing energy. As he waited for the director to call him in, he couldn't seem to sit still, and when I told him my plans for the audition, he stared at me as though I were mad—but mad in an interesting way. What he didn't tell you just now was that I got the lead role in that show and he wound up in the chorus. But John, from that day to this, and for all the days that follow, you will always be my leading man. From this day forward, I will stand by your side. You are the one I will be true to always. Let us make our lives together.

Outline Three

BRIDE:

(Opening verse of a favorite song, or quote from a book or poem that is particularly meaningful to you as a couple.)

GROOM:

(Continuation of this material.)

BRIDE:

(Continuation of this material.)

GROOM:

(Continuation of this material.)

BRIDE:

(Promise or commitment in terms you feel are appropriate for your relationship.)

GROOM:

(Promise or commitment in terms you feel are appropriate for your relationship.)

Example:

BRIDE:

Grow old along with me!

GROOM:

The best is yet to be.

BRIDE:

The last of life, for which the first was made.

GROOM:

Our times are in His hand
Who saith, A whole I planned;
Youth shows but half.
Trust God; see all, nor be afraid!

BRIDE:

God bless our love.

GROOM:

God bless our love.

BRIDE:

John, in this assembly of friends and family,
I take you today as my husband. I do this in
the certainty of my soul, and knowing that
you are my true life partner. I will love you,
honor you, and cherish you for the rest of our
days, so long as we shall live.

GROOM:

Kathy, in this assembly of friends and family,
I take you today as my wife. I do this in the

certainty of my soul, and knowing that you are my true life partner. I will love you, honor you, and cherish you for the rest of our days, so long as we shall live.

Outline Four

BRIDE:
(Dictionary definition of an important aspect of your relationship.)

GROOM:
(Elaboration on this theme, extending into your own interpretation, as a couple, of the word or phrase.)

BRIDE:
(Promise or commitment in terms you feel are appropriate for your relationship.)

GROOM:
(Promise or commitment in terms you feel are appropriate for your relationship.)

Example:

BRIDE:
The dictionary defines love as the attraction or affection felt for a person who elicits delight and admiration.

GROOM:
For us, as we begin our lives together, that definition is only a beginning. We make a

commitment
to our love
today, and
we see it as
a willingness
to give, to
see oneself
through
another, and
to work
together to
make the
best of parts
of ourselves a reality.

BRIDE:

John, my love for you is the foundation upon
which I want to build my life. Take this ring
as a sign of my faith.

GROOM:

Kathy, my love for you is the foundation upon
which I want to build my life. Take this ring
as a sign of my faith.

Outline Five

GROOM:

(Brief statement acknowledging and
celebrating the gathering of friends and
family.)

BRIDE:

(Longer statement continuing this idea.)

GROOM:

(Promise or commitment in terms you feel are appropriate for your relationship.)

BRIDE:

(Promise or commitment in terms you feel are appropriate for your relationship.)

Example:

GROOM:

Today we bring two families together—and celebrate as one family.

BRIDE:

To all who have come with us to mark our union today, we offer our thanks for your help through the years, our embrace for your support over the weeks and months that led to this day, and our promise that, as new members of this new and larger family, we will always be there for you as you have been there for us.

GROOM:

Kathy, in joining my life with yours, I give you all that I am and all that I may become. I give myself to you as your husband.

BRIDE:

John, in joining my life with yours, I give you all that I am and all that I may become. I give myself to you as your wife.

Outline Six

BRIDE:

(Scriptural passage that is particularly meaningful to you as a couple.)

GROOM:

(Continuation of this material.)

BRIDE:

(Continuation of this material.)

GROOM:

(Continuation of this material.)

BRIDE:

(Continuation of this material.)

GROOM:

(Continuation of this material.)

BRIDE:

(Promise or commitment in terms you feel are appropriate for your relationship.)

GROOM:

(Promise or commitment in terms you feel are appropriate for your relationship.)

Example:

GROOM:

From the beginning of creation God made them male and female.

BRIDE:

This is why a man must leave father and mother . . .

GROOM:

. . . and the two
become one
body. They are
no longer two,
therefore, but
one body.

BRIDE:
So then, what
God has united
. . .

GROOM:

. . . man must
not divide.

BRIDE:
John, today, in the gathering of this honored
company, we unite in God's love. I pledge
myself to you as your wife, and will be faithful
to you for all of our days.

GROOM:
Kathy, today, in the gathering of this honored
company, we unite in God's love. I pledge
myself to you as your husband, and will be
faithful to you for all of our days.

Outline Seven

(With your partner, develop a single
paragraph, of whatever length you feel is
appropriate, to be recited by both partners.

The paragraph should draw on the material you have written in answer to the questions on earlier pages.)

Example:
J, (name), take you, (name) to be my (husband/wife). J want to grow old along with you; J want to share the blessings of children and family with you. Today, before these honored guests and beloved family members, J vow to love you and honor you for as long as we both shall live. J vow to respect you, listen to you, and grow with you, through good times and bad times.

Be Creative!
Remember: the right way to compose your own wedding vow is your way. The outlines and examples you have just seen are offered as general guidelines only. Jn customizing your own wedding vows, you are always best advised to let your own imagination be your guide. Develop vows that are meaningful to both you and your partner, that say something unique about your love, and that take the form that best exemplifies the way you envision your new life together.

Jn other chapters of this book, you will find many quotes, poems, and scriptural passages for use in developing your personalized wedding vow. When you have reviewed this material, you may wish to come back to this part of the book to use the following forms as you compose drafts of your vows.

First Draft of Our Wedding Vow

_____

_____

_____

_____

_____

_____

_____

_____

_____

_____

_____

_____

_____

_____

_____

_____

_____

_____

_____

_____

Second Draft of Our Wedding Vow

_____

_____

_____

_____

_____

_____

_____

_____

_____

_____

_____

_____

_____

_____

_____

_____

_____

_____

_____

Third Draft of Our Wedding Vow

_____

_____

_____

_____

_____

_____

_____

_____

_____

_____

_____

_____

_____

_____

_____

_____

_____

_____

_____

CHAPTER 2:
GREAT VERSES OF LOVE

In this chapter, you will find extracts from some of the greatest English poems relating to love and marriage. You may wish to use one or more of these extracts, in conjunction with your answers to the brief questionnaire in Chapter  One, as a starting-point for developing your own vows.

For example, you might decide to use the first extract that appears below, from Burr's "Certainty Enough", by having each partner recite four lines in sequence, and then conclude with something like this:

BRIDE:

John, you are my constant star, the enduring point of light in my life. I give myself to you today for as long as I shall live on this earth.

GROOM:

Kathy, you are the constant source of love and support I have always longed for. I give myself to you today for as long as I shall live on this earth.

Alternatively, you may decide to use a

quote as a supplementary reading during
your wedding ceremony.

> I am not sure that Earth is round
> Nor that the sky is really blue.
> The tale of why the apples fall
> May or may not be true.
> I do not know what makes the tides
> Nor what tomorrow's world may do;
> But I have certainty enough,
> For I am sure of you.
> —Amelia Josephine Burr

❖ ❖ ❖

> Drink to me only with thine eyes,
> And I will pledge with mine;
> Or leave a kiss but in the cup,
> And I'll not look for wine.
> The thirst that from the soul doth rise
> Doth ask a drink divine;
> But might I of Jove's nectar sup,
> I would not change for thine.
> —Ben Jonson

❖ ❖ ❖

> . . . come the wild weather,
> come sleet or come snow,

We will stand by each other,
however it blow.

—Simon Dach

We loved with a love that was more than a
love.

—Edgar Allan Poe

. . . Love is not love
Which alters when it alteration finds,
Or bends with the remover to remove.
O, no! It is an ever-fixed mark,
That looks on tempests and is never
shaken;
It is the star to every wandering bark,
Whose worth's unknown, although his
height be taken.

—William Shakespeare

Love's mysteries in souls do grow,
But yet the body is his book.

—John Donne

Our boat to the waves go free,
By the bending tide, where the curled
   wave breaks,
Like the track of the wind on the white
   snowflakes;
Away, away! 'Tis a path o'er the sea.
           —William Ellery Channing

❖ ❖ ❖

Thou art the star that guides me
Along life's changing sea;
And whate'er fate betides me,
This heart still turns to thee.
           —George P. Morris

❖ ❖ ❖

Now the rite is duly done,
Now the word is spoken,
And the spell has made us one
Which may ne'er be broken.
           —Winthrop Mackworth Praed

❖ ❖ ❖

My fellow, my companion, held most dear,
My soul, my other self, my inward friend.
           —Mary Sidney Herbert

Flesh of my flesh, bone of my bone,
J here, though there, yet both but one.
—Anne Bradstreet

Each shining light above us
Has its own peculiar grace;
But every light of heaven
Js in my darling's face.

—John Hay

Those worlds, for which the conqueror
   sighs,
For me would have no charms:
My only world thy gentle eyes—
My throne thy circling arms!
Oh, yes, so well, so tenderly
Thou'rt loved, adored by me,
Whole realms of light and liberty
Were worthless without thee.

—Thomas Moore

So they lov'd as love in twain
Had the essence but in one;

Two distincts, division none . . .
—William Shakespeare

❖ ❖ ❖

I think true love is never blind,
But rather brings an added light,
An inner vision quick to find
The beauties hid from common sight.

No soul can ever clearly see
Another's highest, noblest part;
Save through the sweet philosophy
And loving wisdom of the heart.
—Phoebe Cary

❖ ❖ ❖

Love is not getting, but giving;
It is goodness, and honor, and peace and
    pure living.
—Henry Van Dyke

❖ ❖ ❖

O, human love! thou spirit given
On Earth, of all we hope in Heaven!
—Edgar Allan Poe

❖ ❖ ❖

Love, all alike, no season knows, nor
    clime,
Nor hours, days, months, which are the
    rags of time.

                   —John Donne

❖ ❖ ❖

My bounty is as boundless as the sea.
My love as deep; the more I give to thee,
The more I have, for both are infinite.
              —William Shakespeare

❖ ❖ ❖

Were you the earth, dear Love, and I the
    skies,
My love should shine on you like to the
    sun,
And look upon you with ten thousand eyes
Till heaven wax'd blind, and till the world
    were done.

            —Joshua Sylvester

❖ ❖ ❖

The violet loves a sunny bank,
The cowslip loves the lea,
The scarlet creeper loves the elm,

But I love—thee.

The sunshine kisses mount and vale,
The stars they kiss the sea,
The west winds kiss the clover bloom,
But I kiss—thee.

The oriole weds his mottled mate,
The lily's bride o the bee;
Heaven's marriage ring is round the
    earth—
Shall I wed thee?

—Bayard Taylor

I wonder, by my troth, what thou and I
    did till we lov'd?
—John Donne

Two human loves make one divine.
                    —Elizabeth Barrett Browning

❖ ❖ ❖

Young bride—a wreath for thee,
Of sweet and gentle flowers;
For wedded love was pure and free
In Eden's happy bowers.

Young bride—a song for thee,
A song of joyous measure,
For thy cup of hope shall be
Filled with honeyed pleasure . . .

Young bride—a prayer for thee,
That all thy hopes possessing,
Thy soul may praise her God and he
May crown thee with His blessing.
                    —Martin Farquhar Tupper

❖ ❖ ❖

One half of me is yours, the other half
    yours—
Mine own, I would say; but if mine, then
    yours,
And so all yours!
                    —William Shakespeare

One heart's enough for me—
One heart to love, adore—
One heart's enough for me—
O, who could wish for more?
The birds that soar above,
And sing their songs on high,
Ask but for one to love,
And therefore should not I?

One pair of eyes to gaze,
One pair of sparkling blue,
In which sweet love betrays
Her form of fairest hue;
One pair of glowing cheeks,
Fresh as the rose and fair,
Whose crimson blush bespeaks
The health that's native there.

One pair of hands to twine
Loves flowers fair and gay,
And form a wreath divine,
Which never can decay;
And this is all I ask,
One gentle form and fair—
Beneath whose smiles to bask
And learn loves sweetness there.

—Auguste Mignon

❖ ❖ ❖

How much do I love thee?
Go ask the deep sea
How many rare gems
In its coral caves be;
Or ask the broad billows,
That ceaselessly roar,
How many bright sands
So they kiss on the shore?
—Mary Ashley Townsend

God hath made nothing single.
—Emily Dickinson

I'll love him more, more
Than e'er wife loved before,
Be the days dark or bright.

—Jean Ingelow

❖ ❖ ❖

Joy, gentle friends! Joy and fresh days of
love
Accompany your hearts!

—William Shakespeare

❖ ❖ ❖

The fountains mingle with the river,
And the rivers with the ocean;
The winds of heaven mix forever,
With a sweet emotion;
Nothing in the world is single;
All things by a law divine

In one another's being mingle;
Why not I with thine?
                    —Percy Bysshe Shelley

❖ ❖ ❖

Love comforteth like sunshine after rain.
                    —William Shakespeare

❖ ❖ ❖

Love to faults is always blind,
Always is to joy inclin'd,
Lawless, wing'd, and unconfin'd,
And breaks all chains from every mind.
                    —William Blake

❖ ❖ ❖

. . . true love is a durable fire,
In the mind ever burning,
Never sick, never old, never dead,
From itself never turning.
                    —Sir Walter Raleigh

❖ ❖ ❖

Love sought is good, but given unsought is
    better.
                    —William Shakespeare

Come live with me and be my love,
And we will all the pleasures prove,
That hills and valleys, dales and fields,
Woods or craggy mountains yield.
—Christopher Marlowe

. . . love me for loves sake, that evermore,
Thou may'st love on, through loves
    eternity.
—Elizabeth Barrett Browning

All love is sweet,
Given or returned. Common as light is
    love,
And its familiar voice wearies not ever.
They who inspire it most are fortunate,
As I am now; but those who feel it most
Are happier still.
—Percy Bysshe Shelley

I know not if I know what true love is,
But if I know, then, if I love not him,
I know there is none other I can love.
—Alfred, Lord Tennyson

That Love is all there is,
Is all we know of Love . . .
—Emily Dickinson

. . . Life with its myriad grasp
Our yearning souls shall clasp
By ceaseless love and still expectant
    wonder;
In bonds that shall endure
Indissolubly sure
Till God in death shall part our paths
    asunder.
—Arthur Penrhyn Stanley

Such is my love, to thee I so belong,
That for thy right myself will bear all
    wrong.
—William Shakespeare

. . . Rarely, rarely, comest thou,
Spirit of Delight!
I love all that thou lovest,
Spirit of Delight!
The fresh Earth in new leaves dressed,
And the starry night;
Autumn evening and the morn
When the golden mists are born.
I love tranquil solitude,
And such society
as is quiet, wise and good;
Between thee and me
What difference? but thou dost possess
The things I seek, not love them less.
—Percy Bysshe Shelley

If love were what the rose is,
And I were like the leaf,
Our lives would grow together
In sad or singing weather,
Blown fields or flowerful closes,
Green pleasures or gray grief;
If love were what the rose is,
And I were like the leaf.
—Algernon Charles Swinburne

❖ ❖ ❖

Love makes those young whom age doth
    chill,
And whom he finds young, keeps young
    still.
—William Cartwright

❖ ❖ ❖

Teacher, tender comrade, wife,
A fellow-farer true through life.
—Robert Louis Stevenson

❖ ❖ ❖

For thy sweet love remember'd such
    wealth brings,
That then I scorn to change my state with
    kings.
—William Shakespeare

❖ ❖ ❖

As dew beneath the wind of morning,
As the sea which whirlwinds waken,
As the birds at thunder's warning,
As aught mute yet deeply shaken,
As one who feels an unseen spirit
Is my heart when thine is near it.

—Percy Bysshe Shelley

❖ ❖ ❖

Grow old along with me!
The best is yet to be.
The last of life, for which the first was
    made.
Our times are in His hand
Who saith, A whole I planned;
Youth shows but half. Trust God; see all,
    nor be afraid!

—Robert Browning

❖ ❖ ❖

How do I love thee? Let me count the
    ways.
I love thee to the depth and breadth and
    height
My soul can reach, when feeling out of
    sight
For the ends of Being and ideal Grace.
I love thee to the level of every day's

Most quiet need, by sun and candle-light.
I love thee freely, as men strive for Right;
I love thee purely, as they turn from
    Praise.
I love thee with the passion put to use
In my old griefs, and with my childhoods
    faith.
I love thee with a love I seemed to lose
With my lost saints—I love thee with the
    breath,
Smiles, tears of all my life!—and if God
    choose,
I shall but love thee better after death.
                    —Elizabeth Barrett Browning

CHAPTER 3:
GREAT THOUGHTS ON
LOVE AND MARRIAGE

In this chapter, you'll find some immortal prose observations on love. These extracts, too, may be helpful to you in developing your personalized wedding vow. A powerful quote can be an excellent way to begin your exchange of vows. Consider this example:

BRIDE:
It's been said that love is space and time—as measured by the heart.
GROOM:
Today, we begin a new life together, united by a love that has transcended distance, a love that will see us through the great journey of a lifetime, the journey through time.
BRIDE:
We undertake that journey together as a new being, no longer two, but one.
GROOM:
Kathy, I offer you my heart, my life, and my faith; may our love be without measure through measureless time.
BRIDE:
John, I offer you my heart, my life, and my

faith; may our love be without measure through measureless time.

❖ ❖ ❖

True love is a durable fire in the mind ever burning.

—Sir Walter Raleigh

❖ ❖ ❖

In our life there is a single color, as on an artist's palette, which provides the meaning of life and art. It is the color of love.

—Marc Chagall

❖ ❖ ❖

Love knows no rule.

—St. Jerome

❖ ❖ ❖

Love is ever the beginning of knowledge, as fire is of light.

—Thomas Carlyle

❖ ❖ ❖

Bitterness imprisons life; love releases it.
Bitterness paralyzes life; love empowers it.
Bitterness sours life; love sweetens it.
Bitterness sickens life; love heals it.
Bitterness blinds life; love anoints its eyes.
—Harry Emerson Fosdick

Oh, what a heaven is love!
—Thomas Dekker

❖ ❖ ❖

Love is the only sane and satisfactory
answer to the problem of human existence.
—Erich Fromm

❖ ❖ ❖

Since love is the most delicate and total act
of a soul, it will reflect the state and nature of

the soul. If the individual is not sensitive, how can his love be sentient? If he is not profound, how can his love be deep? As one is, so is his love.

—José Ortega y Gasset

❖ ❖ ❖

Love and you shall be loved.
—Ralph Waldo Emerson

❖ ❖ ❖

The truth is that there is only one terminal dignity—love. And the story of a love is not important—what is important is that one is capable of love. It is perhaps the only glimpse we are permitted of eternity.

—Helen Hayes

❖ ❖ ❖

Love is immortality.

—Plato

❖ ❖ ❖

Love doesn't just sit there, like a stone; it has to be made, like bread, remade all the time, made new.
—Ursula K. Le Guin

❖ ❖ ❖

Love keeps the cold out better than a cloak.
—Henry Wadsworth Longfellow

You will reciprocally promise love, loyalty, and matrimonial honesty. We only want for you this day that these words constitute the principle of your entire life; that with the help of divine grace you will observe these solemn vows that today, before God, you formulate.
—Pope John Paul II

Hail wedded love, mysterious law, true source of all humanity.

—John Milton

Love conquers all.

—Virgil

The web of marriage is made by propinquity, in the day to day living side by side, looking outward and working outward in the same direction. It is woven in space and in time of the substance of life itself.

—Anne Morrow Lindbergh

❖ ❖ ❖

Only a life lived for another is worthwhile.

—Albert Einstein

❖ ❖ ❖

This is one of the miracles of love: It gives . . . a power of seeing through its own enchantments and yet not being disenchanted.

—C. S. Lewis

❖ ❖ ❖

How vast a memory has love!

—Alexander Pope

❖ ❖ ❖

A successful marriage requires falling in love many times, always with the same person.
—Mignon McLaughlin

❖ ❖ ❖

Love is enough, though the world be waning.
—William Morris

❖ ❖ ❖

Love like ours can never die!
—Rudyard Kipling

❖ ❖ ❖

There is no surprise more magical than the surprise of being loved: It is God's finger on man's shoulder.
—Charles Morgan

❖ ❖ ❖

Love is that splendid triggering of human vitality . . . the supreme activity which nature affords anyone for going out of himself toward someone else.

—José Ortega y Gasset

❖ ❖ ❖

Love vanquishes time. To lovers, a moment can be eternity, and eternity can be the tick of a clock.

—Mary Parrish

❖ ❖ ❖

Love is not weakness. It is strong. Only the sacrament of marriage can contain it.

—Boris Pasternak; from DR. ZHIVAGO, translated by Manya Harari and Max Hayward

❖ ❖ ❖

I would like to have engraved inside every wedding band: Be kind to one another. This is the Golden Rule of marriage and the secret of making love last through the years.
— Randolph Ray

Love is you, you and me.
—John Lennon

Love is an attempt to change a piece of a dream world into reality.
—Theodor Reik

Love does not consist of gazing at each other, but in looking outward together in the same direction.
—Antoine de Saint Exupéry

Loving can cost a lot, but not loving always costs more, and those who fear to love often find that want of love is an emptiness that robs the joy from life.

—Merle Shain

❖ ❖ ❖

To love is to place our happiness in the happiness of another.

—Gottfried Wilhelm von Leibniz

❖ ❖ ❖

When the wedding march sounds the resolute approach, the clock no longer ticks, it tolls the hour . . . The figures in the aisle are no longer individuals. They symbolize the human race.

—Anne Morrow Lindbergh

❖ ❖ ❖

To love and be loved is to feel the sun from both sides.
— David Viscott

❖ ❖ ❖

Love is an energy which exists of itself. It is its own value.
—Thornton Wilder

❖ ❖ ❖

My greatest good fortune in a life of brilliant experiences has been to find you, and to lead my life with you. I don't feel far away from you out here at all. I feel very near in my heart; and also I feel that the nearer I get to honour, the nearer I am to you.
—Winston Churchill, in a letter to his wife

❖ ❖ ❖

Where there is great love there are always miracles.

—Willa Cather

❖ ❖ ❖

Marriage is not a union merely between two creatures—it is a union between two spirits; and the intention of that bond is to perfect the nature of both.

—Frederick William Robertson

Love, indeed, lends a precious seeing to the eye, and hearing to the ear: all sights and sounds are glorified by the light of its presence.

—Frederick Saunders

Until I loved, I was a child.

—Charles Mackay

❖ ❖ ❖

I wish to believe in immortality—I wish to live with you for ever.
　　—John Keats, in a love letter to Fanny Brawne

When you love someone, you love the whole person, just as he or she is, and not as you would like them to be.

　　　　　　　　　　　　　　　—Leo Tolstoi

Your embraces alone give life to my heart.
　　　　　　　　—Ancient Egyptian inscription

For those who love, time is eternity.
　　　　　　　　　　　—Henry Van Dyke

CHAPTER 4:
SCRIPTURAL PASSAGES
YOU MAY WANT TO
INCORPORATE

What follows is a selection of passages appropriate for weddings from holy writings in a number of faiths. Even if yours is a civil or secular proceeding, you may decide that it is appropriate to incorporate one of the following scriptural passages into your ceremony.

If your ceremony is to take place within the context of an established religious tradition, be sure to review your choice of scripture selection with your officiant. Your tradition may require that you follow certain guidelines in choosing verses.

And God blessed them, and God said unto them, Be fruitful, and multiply, and replenish the earth, and subdue it . . .

—Genesis 1:28

How much better is thy love than wine!

—Song of Solomon 4:10

When the one man loves the one woman and the one woman loves the one man, the very angels desert heaven and sit in that house and sing for joy.

—Braham-Sutra

And the Lord God said, It is not good that the man should be alone; I will make him a help mate for him. And out of the ground, the Lord God formed every beast of the field, and every fowl of the air; and brought them unto Adam to see what he would call them: and whatsoever Adam called every living creature, that was the name thereof. And Adam gave names to all cattle, and to the fowl of the air, and to every beast of the field; but for Adam there was not found a help mate for him. And the Lord caused a deep sleep to fall upon Adam, and he slept: and he took one of his ribs, and closed up the flesh instead thereof; and the rib, which the Lord God had taken from the man, made he a woman, and brought her unto the man. And Adam said, This is now bone of my bones, and flesh of my flesh: she shall be called Woman, because she was taken out of Man. Therefore shall a man leave his father and his mother, and shall cleave unto his wife: and they shall be one flesh.

—Genesis 2:18-24

❖ ❖ ❖

From the beginning of creation God made them male and female. For this cause shall a man leave his father and mother, and cleave to his wife; and they twain shall be one flesh: so then they are no more twain, but one flesh. What therefore God hath joined together, let not man put asunder.

—Mark 10:6-9

❖ ❖ ❖

As the Father hath loved me, so have I loved you: continue ye in my love. If ye keep my commandments, ye shall abide in my love; even as I have kept my Father's commandments, and abide in his love. These things have I spoken unto you, that my joy might remain in you, and that your joy might be full. This is my commandment: that ye love one another as I have loved you.

—John 15:9-12

❖ ❖ ❖

The moral man will find the moral law beginning in the relation between husband and wife, but ending only in the vast reaches of the universe.

—Confucius

❖ ❖ ❖

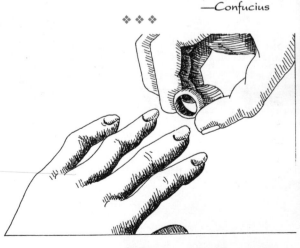

Walk in love, as Christ also hath loved us, and hath given himself for us as an offering and a sacrifice to God for a sweet-smelling savor.

—Ephesians 5:2

Blessed is every one that feareth the Lord; that walketh in his ways. For thou shalt eat the labor of thine hands; happy shalt thou be, and it shall be well with thee. Thy wife shall be as a fruitful vine by the sides of thine house, thy children like olive plants round about thy table. Behold, that thus shall the man be blessed that feareth the Lord.

—Psalm 128:1-4

He brought me to the banqueting house, and his banner over me was love.

— Song of Solomon 2:4

❖ ❖ ❖

I am He, you are She; I am Song, you are Verse; I am Heaven, you are Earth. Together shall we dwell here, becoming parents of children.

— Atharva Veda

❖ ❖ ❖

. . . whither thou goest, I will go; and where thou lodgest, I will lodge; thy people shall be my people, and thy God, my God. Where thou diest, will I die, and there will I be buried . . .

— Ruth 1:16-17

❖ ❖ ❖

Many waters cannot quench love, neither can the floods drown it . . .

— Song of Solomon 8:7

❖ ❖ ❖

Love is patient; love is kind and envies no one. Love is never boastful, nor conceited, nor rude; never selfish, not quick to take offense. Love keeps no score of wrongs; does not gloat over other men's sins, but delights in the truth. There is nothing love cannot face; there is no limit to its faith, its hope, and its endurance.

—1 Corinthians 13:4–7

When two people are at one in their inmost hearts, they shatter even the strength of iron or of bronze.

—The I Ching

Blessed art thou, O Lord, King of the
Universe, who created mirth and joy,
bridegroom and bride, gladness, jubilation,
dancing, and delight, love and brotherhood,
peace and fellowship. Quickly, O Lord our
God, may the sound of mirth and
joy be heard in the
streets of Judah
and Jerusalem,
the voice of
bridegroom and
bride, jubilant
voices of
bridegrooms from
their canopies and
youths from the

feasts of song. Blessed art thou, O Lord,
who makes the bridegroom rejoice with the
bride.

—The Talmud (Ketubot 8a)

❖ ❖ ❖

My beloved spake, and said unto me, Rise
up, my love, my fair one, and come away.
—Song of Solomon 2:10

❖ ❖ ❖

Sweet be the glances we exchange, our faces showing true concord. Enshrine me in thy heart, and let a single spirit dwell within us.

—Atharva Veda

❖ ❖ ❖

Make a joyful noise unto the Lord, all ye lands. Serve the Lord with gladness: come before his presence with singing. Know ye that the Lord he is God: it is he that hath made us, and not we ourselves; we are his people, and the sheep of his pasture. Enter into his gates with thanksgiving, and into his courts with praise: be thankful unto him, and bless his name. For the Lord is good; his mercy is everlasting; and his truth endureth to all generations.

—Psalm 100

❖ ❖ ❖

Only the complete person can love.

—Confucius

❖ ❖ ❖

CHAPTER 5:
THE CLASSIC VOWS

Whether you are marrying in a secular ceremony or a religious one, you may want to review some of the most popular accepted vows. You may decide to use what follows as a framework for use in developing your own vows, whether or not you belong to the tradition in which the vow was developed.

EXTRA EXTRA
Jennifer Andrews
– NOW –
Jennifer Miller
Takes husbands name and thats not all ......

❖ ❖ ❖

I, (name), take thee, (name), to be my wedded (husband/ wife), to have and to hold from this day forward, for better, for worse, for richer, for poorer, in sickness and in health, to love and to cherish, till death do

us part, according to God's holy ordinance;
thereto I plight thee my troth.

—The Book of Common Prayer

❖ ❖ ❖

I, (name), take you, (name), to be my
(husband/wife), and these things I promise
you: I will be faithful to you and honest with
you; I will respect, trust, help, and care for
you; I will share my life with you; I will
forgive you as we have been forgiven; and I
will try with you better to understand
ourselves, the world, and God; through the
best and the worst of what is to come as long
as we live.

—Suggested Lutheran marriage vow

❖ ❖ ❖

GROOM:
In the name of
God, I, (name),
take you, (name),
to be my wife, to
have and to hold
from this day
forward, for
better or worse,
for richer or

poorer, in sickness and in health, to love and to cherish, until we are parted by death. This is my solemn vow.

BRIDE:

In the name of God, I, (name), take you, (name), to be my husband, to have and to hold from this day forward,

for better or worse, for richer or poorer, in sickness and in health, to love and to cherish, until we are parted by death. This is my solemn vow.

—Episcopal Church exchange of vows

❖ ❖ ❖

I, (name), take you, (name), to be my (husband/wife). I promise to be true to you in good times and in bad, in sickness and in health. I will love you and honor you all the days of my life.

I, (name), take you, (name), for my lawful (husband/wife), to have and to hold, from this day forward, for better, for worse, for richer, for poorer, in sickness and in health, until death do us part.

—U.S. alternatives for vows within the Roman Catholic tradition. (If it seems preferable for pastoral reasons, the priest may obtain consent from the couple by asking questions based on the above and receiving the responses, "I do," from each partner.)

❖ ❖ ❖

OFFICIANT:

Christ calls you into union with him and with one another. I ask you now in the presence of God and this congregation to declare your intent. Will you have this man to be your husband, to live together in a holy marriage? Will you love him, comfort

him, honor and keep him in sickness and in health, and forsaking all others, be faithful to him as long as you both shall live?

BRIDE:

I will.

OFFICIANT:

Will you have this woman to be your wife, to live together in a holy marriage? Will you love her, comfort her, honor and keep her in sickness and in health, and forsaking all others, be faithful to her as long as you both shall live?

GROOM:

I will.

—United Methodist Church declaration of consent

❖ ❖ ❖

Behold, you are consecrated unto me with this ring, according to the law of Moses and of Israel.

—In Jewish wedding ceremonies, the groom's words to the bride as he places a wedding ring on her finger after both have drunk from a cup of blessed wine. (Note: betrothal rituals within the Jewish tradition vary widely; the ceremony is usually quite intricate, featuring a number of prayers and blessings.)

❖ ❖ ❖

(Name), I take you to be my lawfully wedded (husband/wife). Before these witnesses I vow to love you and care for you for as long as we both shall live. I take you, with your faults and your strengths, as I offer myself to you with my faults and my

strengths. I will help you when you need help, and turn to you when I need help. I choose you as the person with whom I will spend my life.

—Exchange of vows in standard civil ceremony
(one of many variations)

CHAPTER 6: NONTRADITIONAL VOWS TO USE OR ADAPT

In this part of the book, you will find a number of nontraditional wedding vows meant to be recited by each partner. If you wish, you may use them as written—but if you feel that a measure of personalization is in order, you should certainly feel free to adapt, amend, expand, or delete whatever you see fit. After all, it's your big day!

Today, (name), I join my life to yours, not merely as your (wife/husband), but as your friend, your lover, and your confidant. Let me be the shoulder you lean on, the rock on which you rest, the companion of your life. With you I will walk my path from this day forward.

(Name), with free and unconstrained soul, I give you all I am and all I am to become. Take this ring, and with it my promise of faith, patience, and love, for the rest of my life.

❖ ❖ ❖

I come here today, (name), to join my life to yours before this company. In their presence I pledge to be true to you, to respect you, and to grow with you through the years. Time may pass, fortune may smile, trials may come; no matter what we may encounter together, I vow here that this love will be my only love. I will make my home in your heart from this day forward.

❖ ❖ ❖

What have I to give you, (name)? The promise to take you as

And they lived happily ever after...

my only love from this
day forward, to stand by your
side, to listen when you speak, to comfort you
when you cry, and to join your laughter with
my own. Take this ring, and be my
(husband/wife).

As freely, (name), as God has given me life,
I join my life with yours. Wherever you go, I
will go; whatever you face, I will face. For
good or ill, in happiness or sadness, come
riches or poverty, I take you as my
(husband/wife), and will give myself to no
other.

(Name), you are the one with whom I can share all that I am. Take this ring as a token of my love. Let us live our lives together from this day forward.

To marry the person you have set your heart upon is a joy unparalleled in human life. (Name), take this ring as a sign of my faith and my commitment to our love, and share this joy with me today.

Yesterday, I was separate; today, I join my life with yours. Without hesitation and with full confidence in the step I am taking, I, (name), offer myself to you, (name), as your (husband/wife).

I used to be afraid of falling in love, of giving my heart away. How could I trust a (man/woman) to love me, to give to me all that I wanted to give to (him/her)? (Name), when I met you, I realized how much we could share together. You have renewed my life; today I join that life with yours.

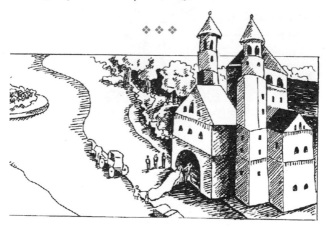

(Name), the words I say to you now are ones I have waited a lifetime to utter, ones I say in love and in confidence. I see in you a strong, growing partner, the person with whom I wish to share my life. I offer you all the days before me, no matter what may come our way. I freely take you as my (husband/wife). Take this ring as a sign of my commitment.

❖ ❖ ❖

(Name), I promise to stand by you, to be there when you need me, and to share the happiness and sadness of my life with you. If the secret of life is to enjoy the passage of time, then let us share our time together from this day forward.

❖ ❖ ❖

Love is something to express, not something to define. (Name), I take today as the opportunity for the fullest expression of my love for you. Here, before these honored guests, I commit to share my life with you as your (husband/wife).

I have only one way, and that is with you. (Name), take this ring, and with it, my love; from this day forward I become your (husband/wife).

A ceremony is for a day; a marriage is for a lifetime. Today, I join my life with yours for as long as I shall live on this earth, forsaking all others. (Name), I freely offer myself to you as your (husband/wife).

Come health, happiness, and prosperity, I will stand with you; come illness, trouble, or poverty, I will stand with you. Take this ring, (name), as a sign of my love and commitment.

Two flames, one light. (Name), I offer you this ring as a sign of life, and myself as your (husband/wife). Let us walk together always, and let us always walk toward the light.

❖ ❖ ❖

I came to this place today as a (man/woman) standing alone; I will walk from it by your side. Today I cross the threshold with you and enter into a new and lasting lifetime commitment. (Name), I commit myself to you as your (husband/wife).

(Name), take this ring as a sign of my love and fidelity. I vow before this company to share my life with you from today onward.

(Name), today we begin our new life together. Let us assume our new roles as marriage partners with love, understanding, trust, and mutual fidelity for as long as we both shall live.

Today, a day of music and celebration, I pledge to share my life with you. Whether the days that come are happy or sad, I will live them with you. (Name), I give myself to you as your (husband/wife).

Love has given us wings, and our journey begins today. (Name), wherever the wind may carry me, I will stay by your side as your (husband/wife). Take this ring as a sign of my love.

Where there has been cold, you have brought warmth; where my life was dark, you have brought light. (Name), I pledge before this assembled company to be your (husband/wife) from this day forward. Let us make of our two lives one life, and let us always honor and respect each other.

❖ ❖ ❖

Love is to be cherished when we find it in life, and I cherish it in you. (Name), let us build a life together. I give myself to you as your (husband/wife), and I pledge here to cherish for all of my days the love we celebrate today.

❖ ❖ ❖

(Name), I am most myself when I am with you. As we begin our life together today, I pledge to respect your unique talents and abilities, and to stand by your side as we grow together over the years. Let us join our lives together and find ourselves anew each day.

❖ ❖ ❖

When I become your (husband/wife) today,
I enter into a new phase of life, and I do so
with joy and with anticipation of the life we
will share together. I pledge before this
honored gathering of friends and family
always to honor and respect our love.
(Name), let us be as one.

Snow falls, but in time it melts; the sun shines,
but in time night falls. Through passing time
and the passing of life, we find meaning only
in bringing joy to another. (Name), join me in
this life, and let us pass winter and summer,
night and day together, from this day
forward.

(Name,) I join my life with yours today without hesitation and with an open and trusting heart. Whatever we may encounter, let us encounter it together. Take this ring, and with it my commitment to be the best (husband/wife) I can be.

(Name), our miracle lies in the path we have chosen together. I enter into this marriage with you knowing that the true magic of love is not to avoid changes, but to navigate them successfully. Let us commit to the miracle of making each day work—together.

❖ ❖ ❖

(Name), I begin my life with you today knowing that we have developed a trust and a commitment that is strong enough to support both good times and bad times. No matter what may come, I pledge to stand by you. May our love deepen and grow with the years, and may we always share in the changes of life with flexibility and respect for each other.

Spring comes, and the grass grows by itself. Love comes, and we act in harmony with all living things to celebrate our love. (Name), today I commit to share my life with you. As we mature as partners, may we always act in full respect of the natural growth and development of our love.

(Name), on this, our wedding day, let us each commit to be partner, lover, companion, and, most importantly, friend. The ride may be easy or it may be rough; let us make it together.

❖ ❖ ❖

I, (name), close one chapter of life and open another today. With you, (name), I commit today to share all that I may be, all that I may become. May each page bear the word of love.

❖ ❖ ❖

(Name), I ask for nothing more from this good life than that I may live out its days with you. I offer here my hand, my heart, and my soul, and trust utterly they will be safe with you. Let us walk as one.

Whatever lies ahead, good or ill, we will face together. Distance may test us for a time, and time may try us. But if we look to each other first, we will always see a friend. (Name), look to me for all the days to come; today I take my place as your (wife/husband).

Today we take the biggest step of all, and yet a step that comes so easily it hardly seems to need a thought to guide it. My natural place, (name), is by your side. Let me remain there for all my days.

❖ ❖ ❖

I saw things indistinctly before our love; today all is clear. (Name), I offer myself to you with all certainty. I should be your (husband/wife) and you should be my (husband/wife). Let us become partners today.

A new dawn, a new day, a new life. This is the first of our days together, (name), and each one will be unique. Let us pledge to each other, before this assembly, to receive each day as the invaluable gift it is, and to always face the dawn together.

❖ ❖ ❖

Now we stand together; may it always be so.
(Name), I offer myself to you today as your
(husband/wife); I will always love you,
respect you, and be faithful to you.

Respecting each other, we commit to live our
lives together for all the days to come.
(Name), I ask you to share this world with
me, for good or for ill. Be my partner, and I
will be yours.

A day together
begins a lifetime
together. (Name), I
offer to share with
you all that I may
encounter, on this
day and on all the
days that follow.

As steady as the tides, our love has borne me along to this day. (Name), you have changed me. I once was alone; now I am whole only with you. Let us join our lives today and, with our hands joined, face the sun and ride all the waves, gentle and strong, that come our way.

(Name), as long as I have this love, I have my home. Today before these honored guests, I pledge to live my life by your side, forsaking all others.

To understand love means to give without a trace of selfishness. (Name), I know we have built a love that will last,

because we have begun to learn to think of "we" first and "I" second. Let us continue to learn this lesson for the rest of our lives— and let our marriage be a sign of what love means to all we meet.

Many of the days that have gone before have been celebrations; but this day is different. Many of the days that have gone before have been accompanied by family and friends; but this day is different. Many of the days that have gone before have been marked with the joy of growth and change; but this day is different. Today J join my life to yours, (name). J do so with a certain and happy heart—on a day that marks the beginning of a new life for us.

Because of the joining of man and woman, we all share in this human life. Today we celebrate this renewal of life; today, (name), J join my life with yours, forsaking all others. Let us live and love, not merely for ourselves, but for the entire human family.

Only the beginning—but the beginning of everything in our new role as life-partners. (Name), take this ring as a sign of my love for you and my commitment to this union. This is the beginning—J will be with you until the end.

❖ ❖ ❖

Jt is amazing when two people find a real love in this world. Jt is amazing to watch that love take root and thrive. Jt is amazing to find yourself in the presence of that love. But when this love has grown strong, (name), as ours has, there is nothing so natural as the decision to commit to that love. J do so here today, and give you all that J am and all that J may become.

The world's storms may storm, and the world's winds may blow, but this love will stay strong. Jt is today, and will be tomorrow, the center of our lives. (Name), J take you as my (husband/wife) from this day forward. Let us live as one in this world.

❖ ❖ ❖

Today we move from "I" to "we". (Name), take this ring as a symbol of my decision to join my life with yours until death should part us. I walked to this place to meet you today; we shall walk from it together.

On this day, (month, day, year), I, (name), join myself to you, (name), before this company. May our days be long, and may they be seasoned with love, understanding, and respect.

CHAPTER 7:
RENEWING YOUR VOWS

In this chapter you will find both completed vows that you may use or adapt in a renewal ceremony, and a number of quotes that may be appropriate for use in your vows.

Vows to Use or Adapt

Perhaps the only thing truer than one's first true love is to recommit to that love before family and friends. (Name), you were and are my love for life—I take you from this day forward as my (husband/wife).

❖ ❖ ❖

Today we marry again, and in every moment of every hour of every day that follows, may we continue to join ourselves in marriage. (Name), with love and joy I recommit myself to this marriage, the central fact of my life.

Once before I have stood with you before family and friends; once again I take your hand as my partner. (Name), I take you this day and for all days as my (husband/wife).

I (name), having found the best part of myself in my life with you, (name), today renew the vows of marriage. May we always walk together in peace and understanding.

The word renaissance means rebirth; today we celebrate the rebirth of our commitment before this honored gathering. (Name), with full confidence in the solid anchor of our love, I take you once again as my (husband/wife).

The act we perform today, we perform with a solemn understanding of the meaning of our love and our commitment. (Name), take this ring as a sign of my renewed commitment to our life together.

I believe in this marriage more strongly than ever. (Name), it is with joy borne of experience and trust that I commit myself once again to be your (husband/wife).

❖ ❖ ❖

To continue in joy, love, and friendship is among the greatest gifts God can bestow on his children. (Name), take this ring as a sign of my undying love for you, and continue with me as we make our way in this world.

J, (name), give to you, (name), a new promise, and yet not so new; a new (husband/wife), and yet not so new; and a new affirmation of love from the heart that has loved you for (number) years and will love you for as many more as God allots to it.

Let us share again the promise we made (number) years ago: to honor and cherish one another, to respect, to listen, and above all, to love before all else. (Name), with joy I promise this to you again today, and again give myself to you as your (husband/wife).

❖ ❖ ❖

Quotes You May Wish to Incorporate into the Ceremony

I love you not only for what you have made of yourself, but for what you are making of me.
—Roy Croft

❖ ❖ ❖

Love is an act of endless forgiveness, a tender look which becomes a habit.
—Peter Ustinov

❖ ❖ ❖

Love cures people, the ones who receive love and the ones who give it, too.
—Karl A. Menninger

❖ ❖ ❖

The bonds of marriage are like any other
bonds—they mature slowly.

—Peter De Vries

❖ ❖ ❖

A successful marriage is an edifice that must
be rebuilt every day.

—Andre Maurois

❖ ❖ ❖

Marriage is that relationship between man
and woman in which the independence is
equal, the dependence mutual, and the
obligation reciprocal.

—L.K. Anspacher

❖ ❖ ❖

The union of
souls will ever be
more perfect
than that of
bodies.

—Erasmus

❖ ❖ ❖

O lay thy hand in mine dear! We're growing old; But Time hath brought no sign, dear, That hearts grow cold. T'is long, long since our new love Made life divine; But age enricheth true love, Like noble wine.
—Gerald Massey

❖ ❖ ❖

Thrice joyous are those united by an unbroken band of love, unsundered by any division before life's final day.

—Horace

❖ ❖ ❖

But happy they, the happiest of their kind, Whom gentler stars unite, and in one fate Their hearts, their fortunes, and their beings blend.

—James Thomson

❖ ❖ ❖

The family is one of
nature's masterpieces.
—George
Santayana

❖ ❖ ❖

Unity, to be real, must
stand the severest
strain without breaking.
—Mahatma Gandhi

❖ ❖ ❖

And Finally . . .

We offer the following poem, a moving tribute
from a husband to a wife during a ceremony
renewing wedding vows. Whether used in its
entirety or excerpted, this can make for a
particularly touching moment during the
ceremony.

The Worn Wedding Ring

Your wedding ring wears thin, dear Wife.
   Ah, summers not a few
  Since I put it on your finger first, have
   passed o'er me and you;
And, Love, what changes we have seen,
   what cares and pleasures, too,
Since you became my own dear wife, when
   this old ring was new!

O, blessings on that
    happy day, the
    happiest of my life,
When, thanks to God,
    your low , sweet
    "Yes" made you my
    loving wife!
Your heart will say the
    same, J know; that
    day's as dear to
    you,
That day that made me
    yours, dear Wife, when this old ring was
    new.

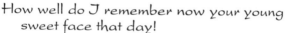

How well do J remember now your young
    sweet face that day!
How fair you were, how dear you were, my
    tongue could hardly say;
Nor how J doted on you: O, how proud J
    was of you!
But did J love you more than now, when
    this old ring was new?

No, no! No fairer were you then than at this
    hour to me;
And, dear as life to me this day, how could
    you dearer be?
As sweet your face might be that day as
    now it is, t'is true;
But did J know your heart as well when this
    old ring was new?

O partner of my gladness, Wife, what care,
   what grief is there
For me you would not bravely face, with me
   you would not share?
O, what a weary want had every day, if
   wanting you,
Wanting the love that God made mine when
   this old ring was new!

Years bring fresh links to bind us, wide,
   young voices that are here;
Young faces round our fire that make their
   mother's yet more dear;
Young loving hearts your care each day
   makes yet more like to you,
More like the loving heart made mine when
   this old ring was new.

And blessed be God! all He has given are
   with us yet; around
Our table every precious life lent to us still
   is found.
Though cares we've known, with hopeful
   hearts the worst we've struggled
   through;
Blessed be His name for all his love since
   this old ring was new!

The past is dear; its sweetness still our
    memories treasure yet;
The griefs we've borne, together borne, we
    would not now forget.
Whatever, Wife, the future brings, heart
    unto heart still true,
We'll share as we have shared all else
    since this old ring was new.

And if God spares us 'mongst our sons and
    daughters to grow old,
We know His goodness will not let your
    heart or mine grow cold;
Your aged eyes will see in mine all they've
    still shown to you,
And mine and yours all they have seen
    since this old ring was new!

And O, when death shall come at last to
    bid me to my rest,
May I die looking in those eyes, and
    resting on that breast;
O, may my parting gaze be blessed with the
    dear sight of you,
Of those fond eyes, fond as they were when
    this old ring was new.

—William Cox Bennett

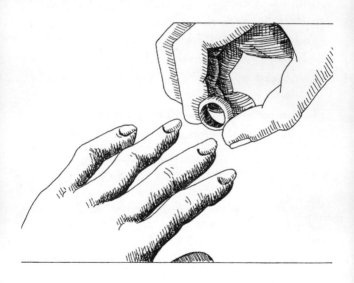

CHAPTER 8:
VOWS FOR SECOND OR
SUBSEQUENT MARRIAGES

The following vows are designed specifically for ceremonies in which one or both partners are marrying for the second or for a subsequent time. (Of course, you may certainly feel free to adapt one of the vows in earlier chapters to your ceremony as you see fit.) After the vows, you will find a number of quotes you may wish to incorporate into the celebration, either as part of your vow or elsewhere in the proceedings.

Vows to Use or Adapt

We come here as two people who know who we are; neither of us could be who we are today, or could offer to share who we will

become tomorrow, without having lived the lives we lived yesterday. (Name), I enter into this marriage with you as an equal partner, secure in the knowledge that we will face our days together with mutual respect. Let us always be willing to grow, to continue to become the people we were meant to be.

I will be your (husband/wife), (name). I will accept you as an independent and equal partner; I will listen to you always; I will respect you and honor you. I am filled with joy that we have found each other.

Since I have found you, (name), I have found a new life. The decision to commit to share that life with you is one I make happily and with full confidence in our love. (Name), let us be husband and wife.

Today we look to the future. (Name), I enter into this marriage with joy and with a firm sense of the importance of sharing our lives as husband and wife. Let us always respect and care for one another from this day forward.

❖ ❖ ❖

Love is not an end result, but a direction. (Name), I offer myself to you as your (husband/wife) because I know that we should make the journey of life together. Let us never fail to speak honestly, to respect each other, and to work to keep ourselves always on a steady course.

(Name), we enter today on a new and unparalleled journey. As your (husband/wife), I will always listen, always respect you, and always work to help us become the best people we can be. Take this ring as a sign of my love for you.

I take you today as my (husband/wife), (name), because it is when I am with you that I feel most complete. Let us join our lives from this day forward.

❖ ❖ ❖

(Name), that I join my life with yours today in complete certainty of heart is the joy of my life. Let us be husband and wife.

❖ ❖ ❖

I, (name), offer myself to you, (name), as your (husband/wife). May we never stop looking to the future, and may we always make time for the present.

❖ ❖ ❖

(Name), I rejoice today in our decision to join our lives. Today, I take my place beside you as your (husband/wife).

❖ ❖ ❖

Quotes You May Wish to Incorporate into the Ceremony

Happiness is not a reward—it is a consequence.
—Robert G. Ingersoll

❖ ❖ ❖

By harmony our souls are swayed;
By harmony the world was made.
—George Granville

❖ ❖ ❖

Life belongs to the living, and he who lives must be prepared for changes.
—Johann Wolfgang von Goethe

❖ ❖ ❖

Happiness is the legal tender of the soul.
—Robert G. Ingersoll

❖ ❖ ❖

In every part and corner of our life, to lose oneself is to be gainer; to forget oneself is to be happy.

—Robert Louis Stevenson

❖ ❖ ❖

Oh Love, love while love lives.

—Ferdinand Freiligrath

❖ ❖ ❖

They alone are wise who know how to love.

—Seneca

❖ ❖ ❖

What we frankly give, forever is our own.

—George Granville

❖ ❖ ❖

Love is a circle, that doth restless move In the same sweet eternity of love.

—Robert Herrick

❖ ❖ ❖

CHAPTER 9:
VOWS FOR PARTICULAR
TIMES OF THE YEAR

In this part of the book, you'll find a customized vow for each month of the year. Whether you use the vow as written or adapt it to your own tastes, of course, is up to you!

January

A new year, a new commitment, and a new chapter in our lives. (Name), I offer myself to you as your (husband/wife), and I pledge to you that I will strive to keep our marriage rooted in the sense of wonder, newness, and uniqueness that we share today in this honored gathering.

February

(Name), we commit ourselves to each other in a time of winter, but the love that brings us here today is the warmest thing I have ever known in my life. I give myself to you as your (husband/wife) from this day forward.

March

BRIDE:

Initially, March was the first month of the year, because it was the first month in which signs of new growth were visible after the ravages of winter.

GROOM:

Today we begin our own new spring together.

BRIDE:

From this day forward, (name), March (date) will mark our new beginning—the first day of our life together as a married couple. On this day, and before these witnesses, I give myself to you as your wife.

GROOM:

From this day forward, (name), March (date) will mark our new beginning—the first day of our life together as a married couple. On this day, and before these witnesses, I give myself to you as your husband.

April

With spring comes rebirth, and with this ceremony we celebrate our new life together. (Name), I take you as my (husband/wife) and vow to honor always the ever-renewing force of life that is the source of our love.

May

The month of May is traditionally a time of dancing, love, and rejoicing. (Name), I rejoice today with friends and family as I offer myself to you for the rest of my days as your (husband/wife).

June

BRIDE:

Some say June was named to honor Juno, the goddess of marriage and fertility.

GROOM:

In her honor, the Romans held a festival on the first day of this enchanting month.

BRIDE:

On this June day, before this honored assembly, (name), I give myself to you as your wife. May our days be many and joyous.

GROOM:

On this June day, before this honored assembly, (name), I give myself to you as your husband. May our days be many and joyous.

July

Now, with summer full in its glory, we join hands and take up our new roles as husband and wife. (Name), I promise to love and be true to

you from this day forward. May our love be as warm and as enduring as the sweetest day of summer.

August

GROOM:

The poet Edmund Spenser described the month of August as "richly arrayed, in garments all of gold."

BRIDE:

Today we formalize and celebrate our union in the company of our friends and family, all of us arrayed in garments befitting the joyous occasion of love confirmed.

GROOM:

(Name), today I offer myself to you as your husband, forsaking all others, and sure of the power of a love as rare as gold and as rich as the fullest day of summer. I will stand by your side forever.

BRIDE:

(Name), today I offer myself to you as your wife, forsaking all others, and sure of the power of a love as rare as gold and as rich as the fullest day of summer. I will stand by your side forever.

September

Today, on the (number) day of the harvest month of September, we reap the bounty of our love, beginning our life together as husband and wife. (Name), I give myself to you as your partner from this day forward, with thanks and with joy as we prepare to share in all the days of love to come.

October

The leaves change and the seasons turn, but our love is constant. (Name), I join my life with yours on this day and for all the days to come. You are the one with whom I choose to spend all the seasons of my life.

November

Today we join our lives by entering formally into the union of marriage. We are thankful indeed to participate in this sacred rite. (Name), I count it as the chief joy of my life on this earth to offer myself to

you today as your (husband/wife).

December

(Name), it is right and fitting that we join as marriage partners at this special time of the year, in the presence of this beloved family and honored friends. I offer myself to you as your (husband/wife); from this day forward, we two shall stand together as one.

And they lived happily ever after...

CHAPTER 10:
THE LAST WORD

By this point, we hope you have enough ideas to develop your own wedding vow—or are comfortable using one of the ones included in this book. At this stage, there remain only two more tasks for us.

The first is to remind you once again to check with your officiant on the requirements of your ceremony. There's no point in falling in love with a particular vow, only to find that it won't be allowed within your tradition. Do yourself a favor by talking with your officiant about everything you have in mind with regard to your wedding vows early

on in the process. Don't save this task for later—you may be in for an unpleasant surprise if your vow does not conform to the requirements of the ceremony in which you'll be participating.

Second, we want to congratulate you on your upcoming wedding—and wish you and your partner all the best in the years ahead!

INDEX

Note: Poems and quotes by particular authors are incorporated here under the author's last name.

Other Adams Media Books

The Everything Wedding Book
by Janet Anastasio and Michelle Bevilacqua
300 pages, illustrations throughout, $12.00

There are hundreds of details to be attended to when it comes to planning the average wedding—and what bride wants her wedding to be average? Wedding experts Janet Anastasio and Michelle Bevilacqua offer insights, advice, menu plans, ceremony suggestions, and dozens upon dozens of detailed charts and lists—in short, everything needed to plan the perfect wedding.

The Everything Wedding Checklist
by Janet Anastasio and Michelle Bevilacqua
144 pages, illustrations throughout, $7.00

From the authors of *The Everything Wedding Book* comes the compact yet completely authoritative listing of all key events and details related to planning a wedding. *The Everything Wedding Checklist* is the last word in wedding checklist guides. It covers hundreds of items—from flower selections to honeymoon preparation, and from printing the invitations to sending thank-you notes.

The Everything Wedding Etiquette Book
by Emily Ehrenstein & Laura Morin
144 pages, illustrations throughout, $7.00

From knowing who to tip—and how much—to dealing with strong-willed bridesmaids, this book is designed to help couples handle even the stickiest wedding issues.

꘏

Available Wherever Books Are Sold